U.S. ARMY RANGER MISSIONS

—A TIMELINE—

by Lisa M. Bolt Simons

CAPSTONE PRESS
a capstone imprint

Blazers Books are published by Capstone Press,
1710 Roe Crest Drive, North Mankato, Minnesota 56003
www.mycapstone.com

Library of Congress Cataloging-in-Publication Data
Simons, Lisa M. B., 1969– author.
U.S. Army Rangers missions : a timeline / by Lisa M. Bolt Simons.
pages cm.—(Blazers. Special Ops mission timelines)
Includes bibliographical references and index.
Summary: "Introduces readers to major special operation missions of the US Army
Rangers in a timeline format"—Provided by publisher.
Audience: Grade 4 to 6.
ISBN 978-1-4914-8701-3 (library binding)
ISBN 978-1-4914-8705-1 (eBook PDF)
1. United States. Army. Ranger Regiment, 75th—History—Juvenile literature. 2. United
States. Army—Commando troops—History—Juvenile literature. I. Title. II. Title:
United States Army Rangers missions.
UA34.R36S56 2016
356'.16740973—dc23   2015026184

Editorial Credits
Aaron Sautter, editor; Kyle Grenz, designer; Jo Miller, media researcher;
Lori Barbeau, production specialist

Capstone Press would like to thank Michael Doidge, Military Historian, for his
assistance in creating this book.

Photo Credits
Corbis: Cpl. P.T. Turner, 21; Getty Images: Archive Photos/Ed Vebell, 9, The LIFE
Picture Collection/Carl Mydans, 19, The LIFE Picture Collection/Eliot Elisofon,
15; Glow Images: Superstock, 7; Granger, NYC - All rights reserved., 13; National
Archives and Records Administration, Cover (top inset); Newscom: Everett Collection,
17, 23, World History Archive, 11; Shutterstock: kanin.studio, Cover (silhouette); U.S.
Air Force photo by Senior Airman Jason Epley, 25; U.S. Army photo by Sgt. Scott
Brooks, 4, Sgt. Teddy Wade, 5, Spc. Nikayla Shodeen, 27, Spc. Steven Hitchcock, 28, 29,
Trish Harris USASOC DCS PAO, Cover (bottom inset)

Design Elements
Getty Images: Photodisc; Shutterstock: ALMAGAMI

Printed in China by Nordica
1015/CA21501403
092015   009210S16

TABLE OF CONTENTS

Expert Survival Skills

U.S. Army Rangers have strong **stealth** and combat skills. These **elite** soldiers have a long history. They have carried out special missions since before the Revolutionary War (1775–1783).

stealth—the ability to move without being detected

elite—describes a group of people who have special skills or talents

French and Indian War

1754–1763

British and American forces fought together during the French and Indian War. They fought French forces and their American Indian **allies**. The Rangers used stealth and **camouflage** to scout and raid enemy forces. They helped defeat France.

ally—a person or country that helps and supports another

camouflage—patterns or colors designed to make military uniforms, gear, and weapons blend in with their surroundings

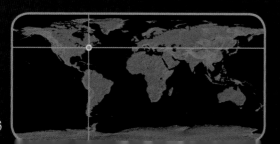

CONFLICT: *AT A GLANCE* **French and Indian War**

1754–1763

Location:
Northeastern colonies and Canada

Mission goal:
increase lands held by Britain

Mission outcome:
French and Indian forces defeated

6

Major Robert Rogers organized the Rogers' Rangers in the mid 1700s. He wrote 28 orders. The Rangers still use 19 of these orders today.

∧ The Rangers often fought on rough ground and in bad weather during the French and Indian War.

1800   1900   2000

The Battles of Saratoga

September 19 and October 7, 1777

In 1777 Morgan's Riflemen fought in two battles against the British at Saratoga, New York. Daniel Morgan led them. The Riflemen used guns that could shoot accurately from a safe distance. The British suffered many **casualties** and had to **surrender**.

casualty—people who are injured, captured, killed, or missing in a battle or war

surrender—to give up or admit defeat

CONFLICT:
AT A GLANCE

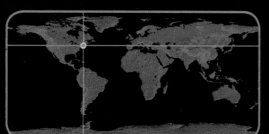

The Battles of Saratoga **Revolutionary War**

Sept. 19 and Oct. 7, 1777

Location:
Saratoga,
New York

Mission goal:
defeat British forces
at Saratoga

Mission outcome:
surrender of British army

In 1775 the Continental Congress formed companies of expert riflemen. In 1777 these companies became known as The Corps of Rangers.

The War of 1812

1812–1815

The U.S. Army trained settlers to become Rangers in the early 1800s. During the War of 1812 (1812–1815), Rangers patrolled the **frontier** on horseback and by boat. They fought in several battles against British and American Indian enemies.

frontier—the far edge of a settled area where few people live

CONFLICT: AT A GLANCE

War of 1812

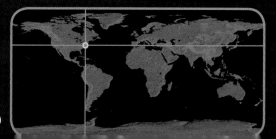

1812–1815

Location:
eastern
United States

Mission goal:
fight British and
Indian forces

Mission outcome:
enemies defeated

Frontiersman Daniel Boone
and President Abraham Lincoln
were both U.S. Rangers.

∧ A large force of American Indians were defeated at the
Battle of Tippecanoe in Indiana on November 7, 1811.

1800   1900   2000

French and   Battles of
Indian War   Saratoga

The U.S. Civil War

1861–1865

During the Civil War, John Singleton Mosby fought for the **Confederacy**. Mosby's Rangers often raided Union camps. They captured Union horses and soldiers. They also destroyed Union railroads. In 1865 Mosby decided to disband his group of Rangers rather than surrender.

Confederacy—the Southern states that fought against the Northern states in the Civil War; also called the Confederate States of America

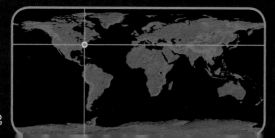

CONFLICT: *AT A GLANCE* **U.S. Civil War**

1861–1865

Location:
Northern states

Mission goal:
defeat Union forces

Mission outcome:
won some battles but lost the war

John Mosby was often called the "Gray Ghost" for his ability to avoid being captured.

⋀ Mosby's Rangers often raided and stole supplies from Union supply lines.

Battle of El Guettar

March 21, 1943

Major William Darby had an important mission in World War II (1939–1945). His 1st Ranger Battalion marched 12 miles (19.3 kilometers) through rough **terrain** in the dark. Then they attacked at dawn. The Rangers captured more than 200 prisoners.

terrain—the surface of the land

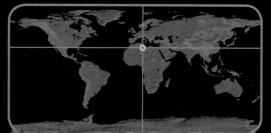

CONFLICT:
AT A GLANCE

Battle of El Guettar World War II

March 21, 1943

Location:
El Guettar,
Tunisia

Mission goal:
capture
El Guettar, Tunisia

Mission outcome:
enemy forces retreat,
captured prisoners

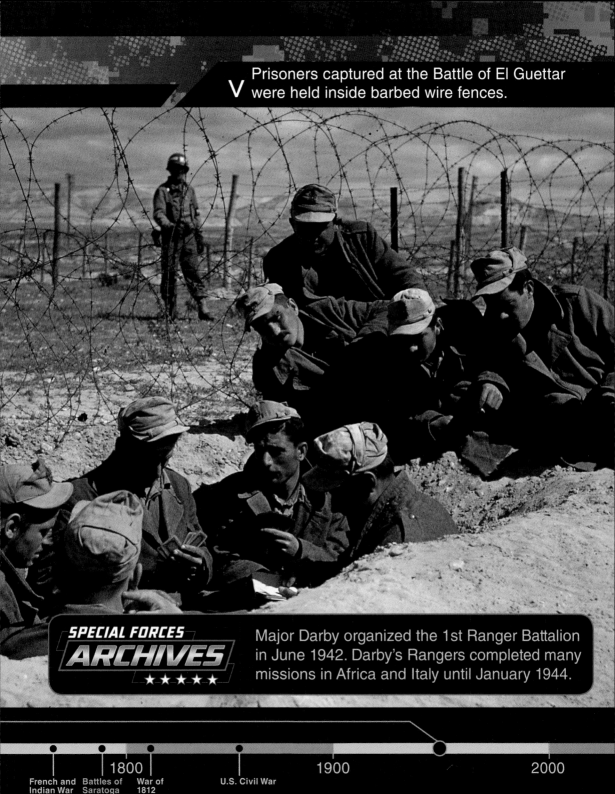

Prisoners captured at the Battle of El Guettar were held inside barbed wire fences.

SPECIAL FORCES ARCHIVES ★★★★★

Major Darby organized the 1st Ranger Battalion in June 1942. Darby's Rangers completed many missions in Africa and Italy until January 1944.

1800   1900   2000

French and Indian War   Battles of Saratoga   War of 1812   U.S. Civil War

The Battle of Normandy

June 6, 1944

The Rangers achieved a key mission during the Battle of Normandy. The soldiers first climbed up 100 foot (30.5 meter) cliffs on rope ladders. They then destroyed German guns to help the **Allies'** invasion of France.

Allies—a group of countries united against Germany during World War II, including France, the United States, Canada, Great Britain, and others

U.S. Rangers climbed steep cliffs at Pointe du Hoc at Omaha Beach to attack German gun positions. >

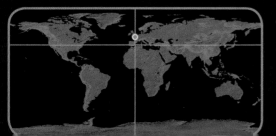

CONFLICT:
AT A GLANCE

The Battle of Normandy

World War II

June 6, 1944

Location:
Normandy,
France

Mission goal:
destroy German
gun positions

Mission outcome:
German guns destroyed,
invasion of France
successful

SPECIAL FORCES
ARCHIVES
★★★★★

The Rangers' daring actions on Omaha Beach inspired their **motto**, "Rangers, lead the way!"

motto—words or a saying that tells what someone believes in or stands for

Raid at Cabanatuan

January 30, 1945

In 1945 the 6th Ranger Battalion joined a special mission. On January 30 they helped raid a Japanese prisoner of war (POW) camp. The soldiers defeated the enemy forces and rescued more than 500 American POWs.

CONFLICT: AT A GLANCE

Raid at Cabanatuan

World War II

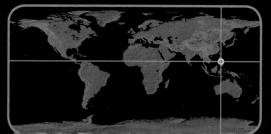

January 30, 1945

Location: Cabanatuan, Philippines

Mission goal: rescue POWs

Mission outcome: rescued POWs and destroyed the camp

U.S. Rangers worked with Filipino soldiers and
other forces during the raid at Cabanatuan.

Operation Tomahawk

March 23, 1951

U.S. Rangers went on a daring mission in the Korean War (1950–1953). First they parachuted behind enemy lines. Then they fought enemy troops before joining other U.S. forces. The Rangers helped the U.S. military advance farther into North Korea.

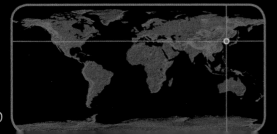

CONFLICT:
AT A GLANCE

Operation
Tomahawk

Korean War

March 23, 1951

Location:
Munsan-ni,
North Korea

Mission goal:
surprise and defeat enemy
forces behind front lines

Mission outcome:
advanced front lines
into enemy territory

SPECIAL FORCES ARCHIVES
★ ★ ★ ★ ★

The 2nd Ranger Infantry Company, Airborne, was the first and last all-African-American Ranger unit in U.S. history. These soldiers were awarded 103 Purple Hearts for their actions in the Korean War.

∧ More than 3,400 soldiers parachuted behind enemy lines during Operation Tomahawk.

1800   1900   2000

French and Indian War   Battles of Saratoga   War of 1812   U.S. Civil War   Battle of El Guettar

Battle of Normandy

Operation Cedar Falls

January 1967

The Rangers were busy during Operation Cedar Falls in the Vietnam War (1959–1975). They destroyed enemy bunkers and searched tunnels. They found and destroyed hidden weapons and other resources. Twice, they **ambushed** enemy forces at night.

ambush—to hide and make a surprise attack

Rangers conducted missions in Vietnam every single day for 43 months. This service is the longest in Ranger history.

French and Indian War | Battles of Saratoga | 1800 | War of 1812 | U.S. Civil War | 1900 | Battle of El Guettar | 2000

Battle of Normandy

Raid at Cabanatuan | Operation Tomahawk

Capture of
H-1 Airfield

March 25, 2003

During the Iraq War (2003–2011),

U.S. Rangers carried out a dramatic mission.

During the night they parachuted onto the

enemy's H-1 airfield in northern Iraq. On the

ground they fought and captured the airfield.

It was later used to launch other missions.

Capture of
H-1 Airfield

Iraq War

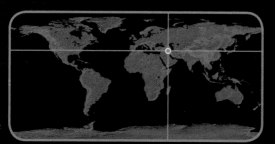

March 25, 2003

Location:
northern Iraq
near Syria

Mission goal:
capture the H-1 airfield

Mission outcome:
airfield captured and
turned into allied
operations base

▼ Some U.S. Rangers practice parachuting at night to carry out nighttime missions.

SPECIAL FORCES ARCHIVES
★ ★ ★ ★ ★

Ranger Special Operations Vehicles (SOVs) are Land Rovers that have been customized and armed.

French and Indian War

Battles of Saratoga

1800

War of 1812

U.S. Civil War

1900

Battle of El Guettar

Battle of Normandy

Raid at Cabanatuan

2000

Operation Cedar Falls

Operation Tomahawk

The War on Terror

July 2006—present

The newest Rangers are called the Regimental Special Troops Battalion (RSTB). These soldiers go on missions to fight and defeat **terrorism** around the world. They perform **reconnaissance**, conduct raids, and carry out rescue operations.

terrorism—the use of threats or force to frighten or harm others

reconnaissance—a mission to gather information about an enemy

CONFLICT: *AT A GLANCE*

Regimental Special Troops Battalion

War on Terror

July 17, 2006 – present

Location:
countries around
the world

Mission goal:
to stop terrorism

Mission outcome:
in progress

∧ RSTB soldiers train hard to be ready for any combat situation.

French and Indian War
Battles of Saratoga
War of 1812
1800
U.S. Civil War
1900
Battle of El Guettar
Battle of Normandy
Raid at Cabanatuan
Operation Cedar Falls
Operation Tomahawk
Capture of H-1 Airfield
2000

Advanced Soldiers

The Rangers have carried out successful missions for more than 250 years. They continue to fight enemies wherever they are found. U.S. Army Rangers are one of the best special operations forces in the world.

.

Glossary

Allies (AL-eyes)—a group of countries united against Germany during World War II, including France, the United States, Canada, Great Britain, and others

ally (AL-eye)—a person or country that helps and supports another

ambush (AM-bush)—to hide and make a surprise attack

camouflage (KA-muh-flahzh)—patterns or colors designed to make military uniforms, gear, and weapons blend in with their surroundings

casualty (KAZH-oo-uhl-tee)—people who are injured, captured, killed, or missing in a battle or war

Confederacy (kuhn-FED-ur-uh-see)—the Southern states that fought against the Northern states in the Civil War; also called the Confederate States of America

elite (i-LEET)—describes a group of people who have special skills or talents

frontier (fruhn-TEER)—the far edge of a settled area where few people live

motto (MOTT-oh)—words or a saying that tells what someone believes in or stands for

reconnaissance (ree-KAH-nuh-suhnss)—a mission to gather information about an enemy

stealth (STELTH)—the ability to move without being detected

surrender (suh-REN-dur)—to give up or admit defeat

terrain (tuh-RAYN)—the surface of the land

terrorism (TER-ur-i-zuhm)—the use of threats or force to frighten or harm others

Read More

Besel, Jennifer M. *The Army Rangers*. Elite Military Forces. Mankato, Minn.: Capstone Press, 2011.

Bozzo, Linda. *Army Rangers*. Serving in the Military. Mankato, Minn.: Amicus High Interest, 2015.

Gordon, Nick. *Army Rangers*. U.S. Military. Minneapolis: Bellwether Media, 2013.

Internet Sites

FactHound offers a safe, fun way to find Internet sites related to this book. All of the sites on FactHound have been researched by our staff.

Here's all you do:

Visit *www.facthound.com*

Type in this code: 9781491487013

Super-cool stuff! Check out projects, games and lots more at
www.capstonekids.com

Critical Thinking Using the Common Core

1. Describe how U.S. Army Rangers use special tactics to achieve their missions. (Key Ideas and Details)

2. Describe in your own words ways that U.S. Army Rangers continue to help people around the world. (Integration of Knowledge and Ideas)

Index